Deep Thinking Can Truly Be Beautiful

MICHELLE TOSTER

authorHOUSE®

AuthorHouse™
1663 Liberty Drive
Bloomington, IN 47403
www.authorhouse.com
Phone: 1 (800) 839-8640

Published by AuthorHouse 09/26/2019

ISBN: 978-1-7283-2757-0 (sc)
ISBN: 978-1-7283-2756-3 (e)

Print information available on the last page.

CONTENTS

ACKNOWLEDGMENTS

This book is dedicated to my mother Lillie Mae Ellis from without her I wouldn't be here today, and also I like to say hello to my children. Anthony, Lakoya, Ahamad they are loved yes always. I didn't forget my better half Mark D. Watson. And last but not lease my two dollar man (Jake).

BY: MICHELLE TOSTER
1989-1991-1992-1993
1994-1995-1996-1997.

NO CHOICE

Comfortable in my ivory tower
barrel lonely, safe hidden shrunken
tiny small and than you suddenly peeking
over my walls.

With fiery eyes and a dazzling smile
I shoved you back and than you called I felt
the lack of aches of your smiles.

I turned again I ran a mile feeling
all your charms and hinges, if I had come
to harm or safety listening for your voice
knowing that I had no choice no other choice
no choice
no choice
no choice.

BY: MICHELLE TOSTER
(a.k.a.) tammy
MAY 5 1992

LONG AND FAR GONE

Slow down read a book because, our
best teachers, are far gone. Move swift
before education don't exist so don't
restrain.

It's been far to long, to long grasp
fast don't let your money, fame and joy
turn to fume for life is like peace long
and, far gone far gone.

BY: MICHELLE TOSTER
(a.k.a.) tammy
AUG 8 1995

2

THE BIRTH MARCH OF MEN

This march of birth was to get back our
immobility
and to authorize our brothers, and sisters to
declare amity.

Which came from the soul, we as a nation have
to acknowledge our worth, peace and pride.

Speak truth, no longer bring silent we're here
to gain back our movements, of the pardon
to be
clear to speak without fear.

This journey was for keepsake we march for
peace,
we march for pride, we won't be denied we
are one man
we are one nation.

We have determination, this empire we have
built
comes with reconciliation, advance my
brothers keep
clear, hold and stand tall, up hold
endurance these things
will give you stability, which brings forth
strong men to
become a monarchy.

BY: MICHELLE TOSTER
(a.k.a.) tammy
OCT 10 1995

A FRIEND NEVER LEAVES

See our GOD
came years, ago
he left us love
from above.

Only he said love
pure, which has no
contamination.

Only a true friend
will do these things
look into the heart
It's knows of no pain
or self gain.

A friend is like
Christ he is the
beginning of the
end and, the end of
thee beginning.

BY: MICHELLE TOSTER
(a.k.a.) tammy
NOV 11 1992

DREAM OF MEETING TWICE

The dream of meeting twice was intense
passionate, and very nice to cross paths
twice
is ecstasy. A myth of hidden species.

Above all the nicest these dreams came with
heavy
emotions such as touch, smell, and feel
wishing that
a mystery which has kept many years truly
has been revealing.

After the dream has stopped what we shared
is extraordinary,
rare, but, yet real to have such a dream.
come true from
details so through and through.

BY: MICHELLE TOSTER
(a.k.a.) tammy
MAY 16 1994

TEARS TEARS

My mama told me that as a
girl that there will come a
time that you'll feel the world's
yours.

She said I'll cry from pain
as you grow up you're smile for
joy but; never did she say I'll cry
for love.

BY: MICHELLE TOSTER
(a.k.a.) tammy
APRIL 10 1993

SNOW FLAKES

Wow It's so bright looking
at you from down and up feel
the breeze that comes with this winds,
winds.

All of them has their own shapes,
and look they totally know where to lay
snow falling slow, so fast.

BY: MICHELLE TOSTER
(a.k.a.) tammy
JAN 10 1996

A LONG LONG CRY

When your soul is
full and your head
is heavy.

Don't think of angry
or pain look up
above say GOD ALLAH.

My father I cry out
bring relief, let me ease my soul
and, release my mind for you bring
forth all that are good and things
that are kind.

BY: MICHELLE TOSTER
(a.k.a.) tammy
AUG 10 1995

FORGIVE ME O LORD

I say father my sins are not
these of my own forgive me
o lord because I've fallen from
your grace.

If I ask for things not of
this world nor do I know thou
know best; maybe I speak wrong
so forgive me.

My LORD and send down your
grace forgive me son of GOD.
FOR THE SINS I'm about to make
I ask for your grace.

BY: MICHELLE TOSTER
(a.k.a.) tammy
MAY 6 1994

PUBLIC ENEMY

It's morning the birds are singing, the
school bell was ringing all the children are
playing
teachers, lawyers, doctors all kind of
people were glad
and gay but; one day out of no where the
enemy came out
some call him war, many say he's drugs most
call him famine
and poverty.

The public enemy is like a omen some kind of
genius he portrays to be a friend; but all
he's doing
is cutting down our population; with guns,
gangs, crime
racism, put him to shame, wake up come a
live bring back
peace and joy back to the hearts and souls
of this here
world.

BY: MICHELLE TOSTER
(a.k.a.) tammy
JAN 17 1991

IF I CAN

How can I find my way back from the place
where you once led me. The harbor, the swing
the lilac, the ring, the promises, the downs,
the dreams.

That you spawned I understand it is all
different now you're a man not a boy but;
a man but; show me my love the way back from
it all and I'll follow your path
if I can
if I can.

BY: MICHELLE TOSTER
(a.k.a.) tammy
FEB 3 1995

UNDERSTANDING

My mother always ask me why I never talk
to her
she just don't know how much I love her and
what I
will do for her; sometimes I try to prove my
love to her
but; it seem what ever I do ain't good
enough.

I still keep trying because I love my mom
Michelle
words can't start to express my love for her
but; what
I need from her is understanding, I want us
to be able to
communicate, and for you to hear what I'm
trying to say is
all I need is understanding from you.

BY: MICHELLE TOSTER
(a.k.a.) tammy
Sept. 16 1996

SOMEDAY

Someday is a place, a time, a dream
a blade of summer grass direct out and
reminiscent
of a day when someday was reality. And
filled with hope
someday was a word we used to taunt each
other.

A distant spot we hungry for, but; were
anxious not to find too soon someday was a
yearning
a man I knew and loved in a someday sort
of way.

BY: MICHELLE TOSTER
(a.k.a.) tammy
FEB 3 1995

FAITH

Do you believe that summer will follow spring
things you can't see don't you know what I
mean
faith's like knowing that there's a pot of
gold
behind a rainbow.

Which your eyes may never behold but; deep
down
inside you know it's real faith comes from
heaven
and it always reveals.

BY: MICHELLE TOSTER
(a.k.a.) tammy
NOV 15 1994

OUR FAMILY STRUGGLE

It started a few hundreds of years ago
in Africa the enemy came and ambush
Kunta Kinte repulse our mother land; then
Nelson Mendela said proudly you can't poison
my mind no matter how much denomination you
force on me. Malcolm X leaves his teachings,
Martin L. King you can read on his
teachings,
don't forget his preachings.

These men knew of the dream, the dream we
shall over come which would bring
deliverance;
the rumor started if we can't get the men
let's
try to over turn the women mother Rosa
Parks of
civil rights movements said the buck stop
here
I'm just as good as you as a matter of
fact I'm
better.

It's your turn to stand mammon for we won't
be come as you are indifferent, scornful we
won't
our ancestors didn't and we all came from
the same family
only one thing has change we're the new
family members
which when we look in the mirror we see
power, we see pride
we won't adjust to their preachings and
teachings.

We have protection we won't be defeated
no longer will we be trapped in the world of
the limited, see we as individuals we are
weak
but; as a family were strong we come direct
were here
to achieve and we will succeed.

Because the devil and his troops are out on
the firing
lines now their losing the game. The war is
over their
whole mission has came to pass we will have
our paradise
in thee end my father and also all my
ancestors said
so.

BY: MICHELLE TOSTER
(a.k.a.) tammy
JAN 23 1995

DEAR MEN STRONG MEN

Men our men
strong living men
true men.

Which from where
you came to where
you're going.

Dear men our
friends our
man our superior.

Yes you dark
and lovely stand
high receive your
prize.

Dear men strong and
gentle men your birth
came from the most high.

BY: MICHELLE TOSTER
(a.k.a.) tammy
AUG 8 1995

DEPENDENT

There was a man from far
South for which he was called
a prince.

Who was adamantine, rare, he had
determination to be dependent he
truly knew by being young when he was
called.

To do his duty, he must be
immoveable, accurate, devoted so
his pride could be happy.

His faith showed him how very
affectionate honest, and bless he
was now he has to learn to be
yare.

So I say for all of these
things you're truly beautiful.

BY: MICHELLE TOSTER
(a.k.a.) tammy
AUG 23 1995

18

ELEVATION

ELEVATION

ELEVATION

Elevate your mind
send your thoughts
up high to the most
high.

Think big, speak strong,
walk tall, sing long,
elevation means most high
far from creation.

And above and beyond
the mind.

BY: MICHELLE TOSTER
(a.k.a.) tammy
FEB 3 1995

ULTIMATELY

So you think so you are
I am wind blowing strong
I am rain pouring hard,
I'm clean, and clear just
like snow.

I am peace full of joy
I am love fill with life
my heart, my eyes, my soul
I'm turned inside out.

I am life I am love I'm
truly peace and joy there for
I think so there for I am this
and this is me ultimately.

BY: MICHELLE TOSTER
(a.k.a.) tammy
JUNE 12 1994

LEARN (NOT) NOT (TO) LOVE

As the heart beats it's hard
to feel this comes easy cause
this is real.

Try not to breath it hurts
don't cry can't why this is
real.

Don't say nothing just look
without joy, or peace can't
why this is real.

What love you can't learn
not to love if this was true
there wouldn't be a world.

So teach and love this must
be learned.

BY: MICHELLE TOSTER
(a.k.a.) tammy
DEC 24 1995

THE WIND

The wind what is the wind
you tell me, I asked you a
question you can possible
see.

The wind can be in any state
of mind it can be of any, many
kinds.

The wind can increase sometimes
you can even possible see and
I say again.

My meaning of the wind is a
cool breeze or warm breeze
flaunting on your body like
a settling breeze.

The wind can be very harsh, or gentle
I don't know about you but I like it
in the middle of the afternoon.

BY: MICHELLE TOSTER
(a.k.a.) tammy
MAY 19 1995

FAMILY PRAYER

Family family
let's fall to our
knees let's pray to our
father through his son.

To stear us clear from
hate, and fear but; at the
same time give us peace
and grant us strength.

Let us hold up our heads high
rest our spirits therefore the
father has called his child home.

Rest your mind cause your
love one is home; yes our savior
of love Christ has redeem his soul
he again said to tell you all.

That we will reunion soon
with Christ.

BY: MICHELLE TOSTER
(a.k.a.) tammy
MAY 18 1989

CLOSE HEARTS

Meeting & passing
when I first saw you
my heart slowed down
but the body felt sudden swift.

To move closer than before
closer, I say closer; as if I
was being pushed and pulled by
a magic force.

My heart beated slower
as if the heart knew of
joy and pain.

Sometimes the heart will
pull a part still even thought
hearts were meant to be broken
the heart knows and holds secrets
of love tokens.

Sometimes near; but the heart is
truly close always deeply within
always close hearts never strays.

BY: MICHELLE TOSTER
(a.k.a.) tammy
JAN 17 1991

A WISH FOR YOU

When you're lonely
I wish you love
when you're down
I wish you joy.

When you're troubled
I'm wishing you peace
when you're sad
just look up.

When things looks empty
I'm wishing you hope
but most of all
I'm wishing you love.

Life and happiness, today
and always, I wish you
could I wish you would
I'm wishing for sure.

The wish you wish come true
I'm wishing for skies so
blue, for love that's true
yes all these good things
I wish for you.

BY: MICHELLE TOSTER
(a.k.a.) tammy
AUG 25 1992

QUESTION A QUESTION?

I ask why this world
is bad? Why don't these
things come to pass?

Why can't sunny days stay
more than four months?
parts of the world never
see as much

Ok why can't we all
be friends? Why must
GOD bring this world
to it's end?

See once more I say
I ask this life I have
will it get better, do I
get witty.

Will the flowers forever
stay pretty? for you see I
don't mean to question but.
without no answers there's only
questions which leaves me with
why ? ? ?

BY: MICHELLE TOSTER
(a.k.a.) tammy
AUG 10 1995

AWAY

Can you see what's no longer
there, where, where I say why
has the trees gone away?

Where has my sun gone away
away, away I'm trying to be
glad and gay but: it's hard.

Especially when everything keep
going away, away I want to go
a far away from here where my
soul can and may run free.

BY: MICHELLE TOSTER
(a.k.a.) tammy
AUG 11 1995

LIES

You said that the sugar
was sweet that the world
was kind; but I know now that you lied.

You said that I'll have peace
and joy someday I'll love forever
but; again you lied, you never said I'll be
come old.

Not once did you said one day
someday I'll be lonely and alone
with no one to love nor hold you lied and I
cried.

Why must things be this way?
Lies lies
more each day
I'll only pray
for better ways
and days.

BY: MICHELLE TOSTER
(a.k.a.) tammy
DEC 3 1994

UNKNOWN PAIN

Children feel that the life
they live is untouch by grief
lovers can't see the untrust.

Fear when they don't come clean
people never stop to think of unknown
pain.

these things come when love don't
come from within.

BY: MICHELLE TOSTER
(a.k.a.) tammy
JAN 14 1997

CATCH A WAVE

Be like a wave, make a loud
roar let your thoughts be heard
from the clap of the waters.

Under the feet climbing high
race long, dig deep, pushing low,
pulled over, be strong, not weak.

for take the strom, the wave will
carry you it will take you far
if knowledge is what you crave.

BY: MICHELLE TOSTER
(a.k.a.) tammy
JAN 15 1997

MOTHER

Mother mother
she is a true savior
see a mom will come or go
to thee ends of the earth.

No path to long no river
to deep, no fire hotter, so
what a mom is to show you she's
a mother a mother, has all and each and
every
details covered.

BY: MICHELLE TOSTER
(a.k.a.) tammy
JAN 18 1997

DON'T LEAVE ME UNSURE

Don't come back tomorrow
to say that the love we know
I didn't think it was pure.

But know this that you can't
play the game I'm not sure if you
leave today, yesterday, will be gone.

And this every and ever lasting
love will be clear nor unclean so
don't leave truly until you're truly
sure.

Look because be true to yourself
and know that this love not for real.

BY: MICHELLE TOSTER
(a.k.a.) tammy
JAN 15 1997

Tasteful Quotes

From

The Soul

BY: MICHELLE TOSTER

CONTENTS

ACKNOWLEDGMENTS

This book is dedicated to my brother Elzie
Ellis Jr. also to my cousin James Martin III
and a uncle Eddie Johnson who are three very
special people whom I really love very much
they take life in more than one spoonful
at a time. Watching them and listening and
learning from them means a lot to me they,
are loved also a very special thanks to two
friends Malikia Davis and Jai Pouge who gave
me a new start in poetry.

To write a book
and not speak of my dad would to be
heartless
because he's my rock in a hard place he told
me that you
can do anything. Thanks dad.

 my brother Corwin
 we will see each other another day
 but until know that your love will
 never
 go untold,

Life may manifest in ways and attest
many things as well (the) (the lovers)
of the world can read between the lines
and almost always find something they can
use in life.

BY: MICHELLE TOSTER

ROSES SO DARK

See my weeping
flower you can't
stand tall you always
lying low.

But your bright
bouquet is busy with
a romantic odor smelling
very good when the wind blow.

Don't be foolish
see the rose can come
in many colors I choose the
dark colors for which their
solid cool and best for all lovers.

BY: MICHELLE TOSTER
(a.k.a.) tammy
8/11/95

MY TREE

Oh my love
first you were a seed
which most friendship needs.

Which must brake the
soil and bloom never to
leave the mind in gloom just
holding on to what has been promising
and new.

Now as the wind blow
your arms move about you can
store many warm and sweet thoughts
of the feeling of love.

You move so swiftly standing
strong and tall proud and butt
most of all you stand in place bold
old stump.

To think you came from
a seed most of all your a
tree a tree for thee my tree you're
the best you could ever be yes I'm happy
you're my tree.

BY: MICHELLE TOSTER
(a.k.a.) tammy
10/10/94

41

A HIDDEN KISS

I found a kiss
which was sweet
moist/but very neat.

A kiss
which comes
complete; and it has it's complex.

I found a kiss
it compares you to
none I've tasted.

Share your lips
with me, cause truly
I've found a kiss that's
a secret a kiss which will
make this wait complete.

BY: MICHELLE TOSTER
(a.k.a.) tammy
6/29/95

A MOIST ROSE

If I remove you from
your roots your juices
will drip then I must
absorbent them.

With my sucker
which has a gentle
soft suction I'll keep
your parts just moist
enough.

By gentle licks, strokes your
love, your love to keep the most
moist I'll lick between your petals.

BY: MICHELLE TOSTER
(a.k.a.) tammy
12/26/94

THE NITE LIGHT

My love let me shine
for you let me be the
light you need see I've seen
the way for which gives us grace
so we can be together true-n-gay.

My love I'm shining bright
not only at nite day light as
well now before you walk putting
one foot in front of thy other just to
remember that the way to stear clear.

Is the means of light in thee
path, so once more my love let me
shine I'll lead don't fall behind
the light for it won't shine.

BY: MICHELLE TOSTER
(a.k.a.) tammy
11/7/95

Love can't always deliver
you, peace however it can teach
you a task as you live and grow.

BY: MICHELLE TOSTER

THE PROMISE

I've made a promise to live and to let live
I promise to love and to be loved to ho,
hold your
hand take long walks on the hot sand play
work cook
sing dance walk halls with you.

And if your world should brake down I'll
be there before you fall I can't promise I'll
never cry but you'll never cry alone I
promise that I
want and need you and us to try I promise
never to play
with your mind but I'll always be there
until the end of
time.

BY: MICHELLE TOSTER
(a.k.a.) tammy
12/29/94

A FEELING OF YOU

In an ant hill
in a tree in a crowd
of sixty three.

I felt lost
and then confused
but you smiled at me
you squeeze my hand.

You hold me close
in your arms you wipe
my tears with you I have no fear.

With you my dear
all I hear is
birds singing.

Only only
a sunny sky
that looks in your
deep brown eyes.

BY: MICHELLE TOSTER
(a.k.a.) tammy
8/25/92

TRUST

I'll always care
why we share that trust
if you say that things are
sweet as sugar I'll believe
cause we have that trust.

I'm close I'm understanding
each and every one of your words
and why cause we have that trust.

My hands heart and soul
I'll put in your hands cause
I know no harm nor wrong will come
to me why why cause we have that
trust.

BY: MICHELLE TOSTER
(a.k.a.) tammy
12/29/95

DESIRABLE

Desirable what can be desirable a lot
of things can be, what do you desire you
can desire life, love, and relationships
success.

You can desire to move on to be the best
you can be desire life, expectation but
desire
if you desire you live to seek knowledge.

BY: MICHELLE TOSTER
(a.k.a.) tammy
8/15/97

SWEET LOVE

Sweet love is what knew to really be looking
for something you won't find behind closed
doors
something that comes from the heart and
within sweet
love also starts out when your just friends.

Sweet love is something everyone needs to
fulfill
their most gratefully dreams all it takes is
something
you and me to make this sweet love become
more than a dream
with a blink of our eyes and a twitch of our
nose we can have
sweet love.

Quicker than a paddle that has fallen off an
rose
no one knows what the future holds but; a
warm blanket when
your cold so come and take this voyage with
me a adventure
of love sweet love, baby.

BY: MICHELLE TOSTER
(a.k.a.) tammy
8/12/98

MY ROSE

My rose not quiet
nor red either
but her beauty
speaks for itself.

A rose a rose
is not just a
flower to me
my vision of
a rose is this.

Short chocolate
skin with a cream
skin tone, eyes that
let you know you need
no one else.

Hands of a green
eye of envy body
of a goddess queen
my rose has all of these things.

BY: MICHELLE TOSTER
(a.k.a.) tammy
12/16/97

* WE MAKE ONE *

Give me your heart
and I'll give you mine
if we really care for each
other in time we'll find out
that we make one.

The things we share
show that we care no longer
do we need to look for that
special someone cause we make
each other complete.

So come with me on this journey
of joy, happiness, romance cause we
make one when we me and you stand.

BY: MICHELLE TOSTER
(a.k.a.) tammy
6/3/98

A TASTEFUL OF LOVE

Fingers, toes, back
legs, arms, ears
these are body parts
you can lick, suck like
a wet juicy kiss from above.

And below your hips
starting at the lips
with a warm soft slippery
movement to slide in and out
yes my touge.

Then twist your door
knobs round and round
and suck me please, rub
my spilt up and down the chest hairs
til they lay down wet and apart, apart.

Then lay you back down on your back stroke
it my way
it's my choice to go hard or slow it's the
banana that
has two nuts will you let me peel your buns
apart and slurp
the joy stick up the neck down the neck of
your scepter so
the rich juices can flow thick and slow.

BY: MICHELLE TOSTER
(a.k.a.) tammy
5/1/96

53

A TIME OF LIFE WITH LOVE

There will come a time
when you must pick right from wrong
this time I'll pick you cause there's
truly no wrong inside of you.

I've found out that your love
has always and will be true when
I'm cold you warm me my heart beats new
when I'm blue then you make my dreams come
true.

You fill my soul and calm down my mind
most of all this time life will be kind.

BY: MICHELLE TOSTER
(a.k.a.) tammy
4/12/92

TRUE THOUGHTS OF YOU

Your love is like a ocean it roams
over and over your soul has shown me
many doors but; must of all it carries
secrets.

Your heart has played tricks on your
head time and time again your kisses brings
tears to my soul which leaves a sweet toll.

Remembering your love making makes
my body weep for more, your smile of joy
brings forth life I look and watch love,
life, unfold.

BY: MICHELLE TOSTER
(a.k.a.) tammy
9/30/98

I'M HERE WHERE THERE HERE WHERE THERE

Hello world it's me I'm here and have been
for a long time but it seems as life has
passed me by or it may have been the other
way around I've been just sitting around oh
look it seem as the trees are all old now
but that's not true I've been here too long
as before if you stand in only one place
you will just see what's in front of you,
my whole life's been one big ball that's
not moving so I must roll it myself there's
things people and places that isn't gonna
come to me so world here I come.

BY: MICHELLE TOSTER
(a.k.a.) tammy
3/30/95

When beauty rise up you learn
that you can speak beauty, you can feel
beauty
maybe wear the beauty, the beauty of it all
we are
all beautiful inside out.

BY: MICHELLE TOSTER

* QUEENS *

QUEENS
what do this
mean.

we are
thee sovereigh
that's right
we're supreme
solid gold.

standing bright
and bold from
fourth which came
fourth from us.

Our nation
which we gave
birth so you see
queens this is what
we mean when we say
respect the black queens
thee black queens.

BY: MICHELLE TOSTER
(a.k.a.) tammy
8/10/95

BEAUTY

What's beauty it's the blooming of the
flowers in the spring
it's the joy of which we love to adorn the
coming of being
beautiful.

The attraction that comes with life's
physical qualities
those glamour beauty spot a patch of
heighten beauty that comes
or becomes what you see's in a beautiful
woman.

The grace in her face the elegance behind
her eyes beauty
comes in the eyes of the be holder.

BY: MICHELLE TOSTER
(a.k.a.) tammy
1/15/95

BLACK AWARENESS

Brothers, sisters
what's wrong is time
is moving too fast

Don't you know
it's black awareness
year the year for bondage
to disperse.

Our women are treated
like harridans the men like
or they act like thralls
wake-up.

We must gait we
have gave them the
upper hand for to long.

Get out that maze
have hell, we measure higher
give yourself recognition.

Sometimes we get boorish
that's because we've been treated
like psycho's weird it's black
awareness year.

The phoney guilty ones
stop now I'm a luminous here
to show my people we are all equal

we qualified I'm tired of talking, until
I'm livid in the face it's black
awareness day.

BY: MICHELLE TOSTER
(a.k.a.) tammy
9/1/95

I SAW YOU

When you came from a far
better than this.

Growing, singing, moving
loving these things came within.

For we are one Africans
that's us Africa queen, queen
of queens from the mother land.

Rich, pure
I say
I saw you
I saw you.

BY: MICHELLE TOSTER
(a.k.a.) tammy
7/7/95

I YOU ME I SEE YOU

Snow in your hair, not of age
warmth in your heart not rage
a smile in your eyes just for
me.

I lean back gentle and you are
my tree your heart has been farer
than mines no longer must you race no
more do you flee or brack date's nor
come home late, your word even sounds great.

You give me the sun, and the moon
in the palm of your hands you need me
you love me you make me cool and calm you
gave me the woman I wanted to be time to
be me
you hold me so gentle and let me feel free
you see.

We stand close together and smile
at our truth you gave me the sun and it's
joy now I'll give you my youth and my love.

BY: MICHELLE TOSTER
(a.k.a.) tammy
7/7/92

BLOOMING

See it started about twenty-one years ago
when you were just a baby I would look into
your eyes and say this world may come to
pass but before this happen "you will have
done great things.

For yourself and others this is the stage
of blooming at two years old you use to
read stories to people around you at four
you would say I'm walking out the door into
school by six people would say she's very
caring.

Then time pass by about ten years by this
point you knew the meaning of being a young
woman you move from jumping rope to nursing
the sick.

Now look you're leaving school with the smile
which will carry you far you have started
to grow just as a young flower in the wild,
just look back and think of the water which
pours over you.

This is what made you and will keep you
growing strong so drink of life juices, take
of the soil do this and grow strong and tall
let no wed envious chop your dreams down
bloom bright bloom my flower never let no
weed chopper weaken your dreams or crops nor
any field hand take your dreams.

BY: MICHELLE TOSTER
(a.k.a.) tammy
2/2/1998

TO MAKE LOVE

We will someday be free
to make love under a tree
to fill and touch to be free.

Say can we make love
in the pool, where it's
nice and cool.

Yes will we make it in the park
long after dark, will we make love
in our house.

On the couch, then to the floor
through a door no we won't be bored
it's time to make love in the bed after
all this is where nothing else needs to be
said.

Til our eyes turn red truly
till our lips sweel, our souls will
cry out we will end up in heaven or hell.

The soul will say at last
we have reached the goal for which
the soul is free and this means we have
truly made love.

BY: MICHELLE TOSTER
(a.k.a.) tammy
12/3/93

MY LOVE COMES WALKING

My love comes walking
and these flowers that never saw
him til this day look, up but then bend
down straightway.

My love sees nothing here
but you who never trembled, this before
and glances down lest I do more.

My love is laughing those
wild things were never tame until I too
down-dropping kissed his silvery shoes.

BY: MICHELLE TOSTER
(a.k.a.) tammy
1/4/94

* MESMERIZE *

In remembrance as a child
how a girl looks back on how
she loved her doll, she had as a child.

The boy I knew as a child
holds more meanings then a childhood
toy, most girls hang on to these things that
brought them joys which comes and brings
when you're a child.

These things that makes me
smile the look in his eyes, the way his back
sway
the smile, on his face that's most of all the
feelings of the
joy and peace that came from his soul.

If you ask me what were the good old days
I would have to say the time when a person
could
be his or her selves or when you could feel
free completely
without fear or pain.

To that boy who swindled the soul for which
I had no control his soul was pure and rich,
of joy and love
and there came a day when this boy joy and
love vanish.

The sun no longer shines this is when he
took away all that
was mines, his smile, his grace, his warm
embrace now there's
only that dream which holds a faded picture
there were times

I could recall when this boy would show me love.

So I looked in books people nor tv showed me how to help this
dent love but what and far most all this
dream needed for realistic
love so his true love could shine completely.

BY: MICHELLE TOSTER
(a.k.a.) tammy
11/5/98

To recognize that there's a place
subsequently death, some may shy away from
it other may await to see where and who they
may go and become.

BY: MICHELLE TOSTER

THE AFTER SHOCK

To wake up am any time after 12 midnite
and say I think this is a good day to die.

You weep trying to speak but all you feel
and hear is a noise.

Then you realize that you have spilt
your soul from your mind.

The after shock now it's time to face up
cause this cup for which you has spill most
of it's duration, now bring reactions pain,
grieve, sorrow
now all that's left is to call for you
father.

BY: MICHELLE TOSTER
(a.k.a.) tammy
1/29/99

70

MY NEW HOME

To my children
To my family
Hold your head up high
Keep your eyes on the sky.

Think clear, think sure
Because my soul is now
Truly pure I go with love
I leave with pride.

I ride that cloud
Way up high, rejoice
Feel free for this place
I reside holds most high
The best gift in the world.

To know that I'm home
With my father so don't
Weep you'll see me again
Remember to look up;
My heart is high in that
Home land high in the sky.

BY: MICHELLE TOSTER
(a.k.a.) tammy
8/8/97

MISSING YOU (BUT YOU'RE STILL HERE)

I know you reside in your new home
where you're rejoicing with the Lord.

And yet you're still here you're
in the waves of the roaring river,
you're in the air we breath.

Yes you're in each family member
by the way we walk, talk, and speak.

So when I'm missing you I'll remember
that the shell is easy to part with but,
the soul will always remain and I'll look
up onto the clouds and guess which one
you're
on and wave hi gone but; still here, truly
were missing
you but we know that you are here.

BY: MICHELLE TOSTER
(a.k.a.) tammy
6/6/98

Neither out (to) far nor in (to) Deep

Drowing in a sea of sinful things
out on a branch, with the bills stick
out your hand he's there.

Have you had a death in the family
maybe can't keep peace in your home
stick out your hands he's there.

The more you fight the tired you get
after all life's ups and downs you though
you had this beat stick out your hands he's
always there any where and every where.

BY: MICHELLE TOSTER
(a.k.a.) tammy
8/13/95

DIVINE ANGEL

See God crated man with hearts of joy and
pure
so to have a friend which comes from above
with
unconditional love.

You must first look in the heart this will
help
share and care he or she knows no harm for
which
the words thee speak.

This diving angel comes with special love
sharing and caring, sounds soft and I'll be
there
I'm here for eternally.

BY: MICHELLE TOSTER
(a.k.a.) tammy
1/16/95

LOST IN HEAVEN

I want to be lost in heaven with all the
angels,
my mind, my soul will become lost with those
songs,
I'll love to sit near the throne; where the
seat of the
king resides

After the resurrection I'll see if one of
them will be me
lost in heaven is where I want to be with
thee.

BY: MICHELLE TOSTER
(a.k.a.) tammy
5/6/91

TODAY

Today today is not here to stay
but today wasn't like yesterday and if I live
to see another just like this one still it
will
not be the same as today.

Because yesterday will either leave or bring
things that wasn't there today before today
like
rain, snow, hale but; in all I'll think of
today yesterday
tomorrow, and next week.

With love and all these days that we shared
each day brings a new start for us.

BY: MICHELLE TOSTER
(a.k.a.) tammy
12/12/94

EMPIRE

Some say the world
will end in fire I
say pray to keep my
soul desire.

Some say the world
will end by fire this
empire will end in fire.

Some say in ice
because people think
It's easy to hate It
also great to be nice.

But if I had to
perish twice I wouldn't
want my empire doomed by
fire nor ice.

BY: MICHELLE TOSTER
(a.k.a.) tammy
3/3/95

77

FEELING FATHER LESS

Today was a good day
I went done to the river, and as I was
walking I seen a green
car like my dad's yes this was a good day to
see my father but;
as always he didn't, couldn't be there for me
yes, today would have
been a good day to see my dad.

I wanted the river to watch me
as it roll over and over just like my dad
his life has been
so unsure it makes one wonder if this is
where your DNA comes
from mama use to say people can't understand
the where abouts
of the soul try to think of love.

But instead all there is a waveless wave
with no sense
a river roaring about like an sleepless
sheet of silk with
no sense of peace, or direction, see it
started when I was walking
when I was young all I saw was a worthless
useless no sense of
respect for others can't be or beat the river
it runs fast.

The river runs slow, never "never you will
never know when
it will change me myself I'm always looking
for a chance it
was a good day to see my dad he was not sure
I don't think as

far as far as love goes he don't know what it
mean.

Dad had to choose the river
over the pond, but; of course he wanted to
be a big fish instead
of a little guppie, fish by the way I ask
why roll over with the
river when you can soak in the pond.

So as I walk the streets, drive the blocks,
look over the river
shop at the stores, talk to people I say
maybe one day I'll be
looking at the river for my dad because, I
can't see him any
where else.

Mama "mama would say the river child is the
place where we
use to go walking, into the grass and a
swimming at the beach
fishing in the river rolling in the grass
but; all we have is to
think of the river.

The river each day I walk down to the river
about 7am to 10am
looking up in the skies, hoping a man walk
aside me and say hey
I said is this my child who a waits by the
river to see a father
that can show her the way to go.

But like dad's they come a dime a dozen just
here to move
with a useless wave, dishonest trust, a long
time endless speech
a non sense lie, but; most of all a no
return address, letter

non love most people would say what do you
get from a walk to
the river each day and this is what I would
say it's the walk
along it's not just to look over the river
nor over the skies or
in between the trees which surrounds all
these things.

See the river brings many things and at the
same time
it can take back others as well as for me
each wave brings me
a special kind of joy a new sound it speak
to me in ways I understand.

By night the river will carrie out all your
sorrows, just drop
your soul into it yes by day can talk to the
river and say today
would have should, have could have, been a
great day to see my dad
but instead I only have the river, today and
tomorrow I guess the
river may speak to me and say don't worry my
child for each day you
walk down to the river your father was by
your side and even when
your not over looking the river child your
father as always been
there.

A father is all you needed and is all and
always what you
have had all your life; so go to the river,
pray at the river, talk
at the river, sing at the river, play at the
river, dance at the river,
and read at the river and read my words at
the river.

Do all these things, when doing these things
remember that I
put the river, the sea, the ocean and all
good things here for
you and now take a walk each day and love
your self child because
for my thoughts can run clear.
run clear, run clear
clear"
Your father truly loves you and this is what
I go to the river
for my thoughts can run clear. And my mind
can feel the vim from
the blue skies, on a clear day and a breeze
which comes from a
gentle wave at the river's bay.

BY: MICHELLE TOSTER
(a.k.a.) tammy
5/10/98

HOME

Home is a place where there is love and
affection
right in your direction, home is a place
where you should
be excepted even if there is something in
your past, your
past and where a family's love can last.

A home is different than a house a house is
just
somewhere you love to live and lay down to
sleep and eat
go to bath or a place you can go if you have
no where else
to go.

A home is a place where you live learn and
love
some place you can go and people will say
forget your
past, let's start to work on the future or
the present,
a home is a place where there's love and
affection.

Special thanks to
my son Ahamad.

BY: MICHELLE TOSTER
(a.k.a.) tammy
8/10/95

SEAS SEAS

Waves, waves
that's all I see
clear across the seas.

You ask me
what I see when
I see that cool, calm
deep blue sea.

I think of
God love his
grace I say Lord
what a beautiful place.

BY: MICHELLE TOSTER
(a.k.a.) tammy
9/1/95

BEHOLD MY SPECIAL ROSE

For which you came
from a seed planted
by God's love and grace.

Yes you bloomed
year after year, you
it was your voice my ears
heard.

I knew you were here
your faith and pride
has gave us hope.

See once your soul
became rerooted into
God's soil I knew that
your life and soul soars
high.

So when I see
the birth of a rose
I will pay attention
and I will know this is your
way of saying hello.

BY: MICHELLE TOSTER
(a.k.a.) tammy
1/8/99

```
     *  MY  LUCK  JOY  OF  LOVE  *
```
```
     *  MY  LUCK  JOY  OF  LOVE  *
```

Most would say luck
that's a state of mind
if you ask me I'll say
it was fate.

Just one look in your eyes
those deep brown sexy eyes
was all it took, "it was as if
I was hooked.

The arch of the essence
from the smile you wear
on your face, the gentle
touch from your hands.

To have missed a lucky love
of peace and joy is like not to haved
at all.

I say your laughter
in my ears makes me feel
like my soul can drift away
within a swift soaring breeze.

So my luck love pour your
charms over thy heart for to hold and keep
all this joy to
yourself.

Is too never feel totally replete
the feeling of connecting with a joy my
love joy

for which my happiness is a mystery left to
be unfold for
which some day truly will be told.

BY: MICHELLE TOSTER
(a.k.a.) tammy
5/19/99

TAKE IN OF LIFE MASSAGES

Sitting on the banks of the river
the Detroit river at that watching
the tides and waves row in and out
one would think of how the world moves by
just like a swift tide.

Looking at the boats, the ships
most of all the people who just seem to be
having a great
time not thinking of the surrounding about
them, just laughing
singing with pride.

I say how sad that no one
takes the time to look around
up, down, to thank the Lord of his goodness
and his joys.

Then a day come when most
will say hey I don't remember
that tree nor did I ever see that light
house standing
over there just as these things appear your
love for life
start to pours.

Nevertheless but; as one walk the roads of
life
he, she, must pass that path to roll with the
waves or stand
as a ship anchor.

Remember that the river is always rooling
over and in and out just keeping it's mind
on one

thing which is to keep moving before it
become as a person
in life at a stand still.

Sometimes being unmoveable
is good at or you can become
stuck so just remember to take on a wave,
roll with fear keep
smiling and stay proud cause everything,
every place, some where
and at some point and time there will be a
river to retrace so
let life massages of life reveal.

BY: MICHELLE TOSTER
(a.k.a.) tammy
4/8/98

* LOVE FOR MY CHILDREN *

I know life has had it's hurts
but; as always the day will come
when you can say that mama you made away
when there was no way.

Maybe not today
maybe not years to come but; mark my words,
for today
there will be a place and time that will
tell the story.

See my children mama
has a great dream for you
you must, all of you this is something
which you
must do and the paths you choose will take
you far.

But you should know if there was ever
a time, place or thing which will stand in
your way
mama will do her best to move any thing that
keeps mama child
from moving up the road, to becoming a prize
trophy.

What I'm trying to say
is your are my everything my mama use to say
mama
will make a way out of no way, so when times
become to hard
just remember you have a love that can stand
the stand, and
nothing can touch this, mama's have the pull
that can bring
you back in from the storm.

This love is the love that's a mother love
which bares
already winner, you're a winner my child
cause I won't let
you fail, no way no how the road is long,
the skies are cloudy
but your a winner and you'll come out just
alright.

BY: MICHELLE TOSTER
(a.k.a.) tammy
5/28/99

BORROWED
      time
         that's
            taken
               for
                  granted

People walking
around with hate
instead of love.

Because each
nite stars turns
to morning skies.

Summer heats
needs fall
winds to blow.

Spring may never
come again if
there wasn't winter.

I don't mean that
things will remain
the same.

Time running out
you can't live in sorrow
our time is borrowed.

BY: MICHELLE TOSTER
(a.k.a.) tammy
4/18/93

NOTHING LIKE THE RAIN

Nothing like the rain
nothing like the rain.

The rain can come
and go but; the
rain never stay.

Never stay gone, sometimes
it has a steady but; constant
flow.

The rain can go
fast the rain can go slow.

But! it never stay
and never stay gone
thr rain can come today and come
back next week.

And it also can come
from the stomp of God's feet.

Or the flick of his rist
or the grasp of his hands
or the twitch of his head.

Or even the slight thoughts
of God mind once and each and everytime.

Like I said once
before there's nothing
like the rain.

BY: MICHELLE TOSTER
(a.k.a.) tammy
8/10/95

As I would like to thank
a special person: ahamad

BE NOT SORRY FOR WORK TOWARD TOMORROW

I use to be afraid
of all things that I couldn't
control but; a day came when my Lord said.

Let not your soul
fear cause I put all things
in order pray my child, cry until the soul
pour out joy of red.

I use to cry a lot
jump around and say why me
Lord things can't get any worse.

Then I heard of the things
and times in other places and time.

Ho I said what sorrows
I have are not as bad but; if
I don't get my soul right by tomorrow
the oh sorrows will all be mine.

This wasn't fine with me
so I ask myself what can I do
"do this a voice said" be kind, use
each day as it or if it was your last.

Pray be kind take time
to share a good word or two give
a helping hand when needee, do all these
things and in time

your soul will be rewarded with the joys of
tomorrow.

BY: MICHELLE TOSTER
(a.k.a.) tammy
5/15/93

WAITING TO SEE

I wait each nite
to see if he will come.

And time again he
shows up to calm my soul.

See he starts out
with a bright red-orange
then it seem red-yellow.

My friend the sun
has took me home once more
I wait.

To see if the next day
he'll come to move my spirits.

Yes I wait everyday
in and evening out just to see
him evanescent into the skies.

So once more I wait
with my eyes glued to the sky.

BY: MICHELLE TOSTER
(a.k.a.) tammy
3/18/96

These poems come from the inner soul
just to let your mind flow on many points of
views.

NEVER SAY SORRY

I'll never say
I'm sorry even
after I've taken
that last bend.

Then say I'm
still not sorry
cause I have learned.

To love to
understand, to care,
to share so there forgive.

If you have
it to give or to spare
we can't always do right.

If you can think of life
Life sometimes seems unreal
cause life, love always reveals.

BY: MICHELLE TOSTER
(a.k.a.) tammy
2/5/95

MAKE A MOVE

Pull the door
open can't get
my knees unlock
to move about.

To open the gates
to open the shades
to find that bars on windows
looking at you.

Your eyes bare
fear which deeply
hidden inside, strongly
wanting to come out side.

Hey it's dark
down in your souls
afraid to love, behold
release.

Become free
don't worry
it's still time
to have peace.

BY: MICHELLE TOSTER
(a.k.a.) tammy
12/28/94

QUOTES FROM THE SOUL IS A BOOK
FOR EVERYONE OF ALL AGES TO READ THIS BOOK
CAN OPEN UP THE
MINDS"! OF ANY LIKENESS,

From my experience of my life and as well for love we all can sit down and tell a story or too I just would like you to enjoy the words from my heart and try to remember a time where one of these poems, can take you. And don't forget the lord, for he will always be there, hope this book can be read in many places such as schools, homes plays any where the feeling should hit.

EMPTINESS

Darkness of a empty
room, which holds nothing but; gloom.

Things don't have feelings
words without emotions are
just like shells without sand.

Tap a tree that sounds
hollow which all this was
too hard too swallow.

These things are vacant
which leaves the heart aching.

Have you ever opened
a book, nothing inside see
this is what you call empty pride.

BY: MICHELLE TOSTER
(a.k.a.) tammy
2/5/95

A MOON APART

Living in the same city
in the same state, but
yet two or more moons apart.

Your mind and hearts
can't seem to pick up
the wave even after all you try to be brave.

I'm your bride, you're
my groom still all and all
we're just a moon apart.

Keep the faith be strong
the mood is there here for me
there for you I'm here "you're
there just a moon apart.

BY: MICHELLE TOSTER
(a.k.a.) tammy
12/29/95

WASH & DRY

People do you wrong
that's a cold wash
you cry then wipe your eyes
nice clean and dry.

Lose all your pride
then be kicked to roads sides.

Move up and hold your head
high, your born in this world
young and then some leave it old.

Other's leave it hard
and cold, wash-n-dry,
keep your head high.

So I've been told
grab the world and take
a hold.

BY: MICHELLE TOSTER
(a.k.a.) tammy
3/12/94

RETHINK IT

Do you look at me
because there's no other
face? do you call me your
long loss? but; peaceful joy and grace.

Why don't u want to look
beyond my mind, to see if love
from me, "me couldn't get you hooked.

Which son will you choose
or just would you prefer to have
a boy or a girl? to love that's pure.

I'm still not sure
which one is it your mind
your heart that's cool, clod, cloudy not sure
and clear.

Baby "baby time that hasn't
stood still sometimes, brings
about things that not real, you
walkon to fall over.

One day to see that what you
have waited for is just the darkness
once you uncover this hood be not hopeful
but sure.

BY: MICHELLE TOSTER
(a.k.a.) tammy
4/17/96

THE VACANT ROOM

The vacant room
behind the door there's
only walls, halls, wait.

I hear a call
it says come in please
my empty room please.

Cause I'll only accumble
dust, dust, I say, my room
is vacant now if you stay.

This room may become
bright, and gay, for where
there's room to fill there's
room to build.

The winds can
no longer blow
in cold air, air
nor the floor will
crack, the room will
glow from wall to wall
a wall and all that
that comes in will
flow, clean throught
this vacant room.

BY: MICHELLE TOSTER
(a.k.a.) tammy
1/17/91

WHEN SOULS KEEP MOVING APART
BUT THE HEART WILL DEATHLY STAND

When I look over the years
to see how many tears we have lost, I use
to say what's wrong with this picture; then
I sit while
my mind and heart drift in the clouds, but
when too much time
has passed on I find out that the long
painful and forgotten
roads.

To the new life, or the soul mender this is
what I call life
a new you a new me, see in order to start a
new you must
shead off the old the unwanted things.

And the most amazing out come of it all
is to know that the journey; to come will
bring
forth peace, and joy also potential, because
without hope
of a new beginning you can only butt in and
bluff your way
then what will become of this, will feelings
or acts? of the
long blue depressed advantages.

Time and time again what's the most
important things, pray for a place in your
world use your

heart cause the mind tends to let you feel
untrue feelings.

BY: MICHELLE TOSTER
(a.k.a.) tammy
1/27/99

A BEAUTIFUL LOVE

Beauty is in the eyes
of the beholder, one could
look at a tree "a tree" which
all that was left eee! was a stomp
and you may said that's true beauty.

A beautiful love
when your blue a love of
a friend can light up your heart
with rays from a rainbow, that makes your
soul dance across the sky.

A beautiful love
a beautiful love
today, tomorrow am.pm love always
a good thing and people coming together, it's
that
special togetherness.

See love it's a wonderful admiration
I would like to send out my deepest
appreciation
it's good to know I'm from a family which
sends out beauty.

BY: MICHELLE TOSTER
(a.k.a.) tammy
6/1/99

SISTERS SISTERS

Geraldine
you're the oldest
and worth comes from the deepest center
of your heart, of the world which is the
world's most
loved which is the snow white pearl.

Carenia
yes you comes in at third
but, there's a time when your hurom
and witts, becomes most aware, because of
the sense of caring
comes from the love you share.

Sarah
you're fouth
in line, even through you're love and trust
is like a heart of gold which always comes
in first.

Nioka
the last but, not never forgotten
you're quite, cute, and we all adore you
the gift you share is like the youth of age
and the soul of rage but, your life has all
of our pages
unfolding in you. The style, the grace so to
you hold your
head high keep the pace cause your life will
find that special
place, but, remember that until and even
when it do you will always
have a spot in my soul, your heart is our
heart we beat as one.

BROTHERS BROTHERS

LEE_Lee
you're my big brother
also my family soul mate
to me you bring life meaning
cause you make all hard things happen
your faith comes from the most high so to
you my brother you're the best in this God
made world.

Michael
see when I think
of you I see the live and let live
spirit which most wish they could bring
forth, you maybe number two but, you see
there's many who wish
they knew how to become like you.

James
the amazing
you're a tool for which you
have created many priceless discovers
the charm you throw off let's one know
they are lucky to have you as a brother.

Jerome
you're the baby boy
so you must keep us on our toes, by
being our
ambassador for u we don't envoy all we wish
to look down
on you to say to that special you, stand-up
for you're our
brother and we can stand tall.

So after all this has been said by the
number two sister

Michelle we are alick, a kiss, a dream so I
say we and entity
which emphatic so to my better halves, stay
positive cause your
are loved thanks mom for giving me the best
of life's gifts
and joys. A family a loving family.

BY: MICHELLE TOSTER
(a.k.a.) tammy
5/25/98

MY EMBROIDER

Lee after all the rude turmoils
and many back lashes, still you have move
forward and toward promotion.

MY precious
work of art, congratulations
you were able to stay clear of the
world's untrue Illusions.

So embed your pattern
just weave on and hold and take
God's thread for this will last
and the lost heart, old wounds, harsh words
these things will come to pass.

Your soul is like endless time
you'll always be remember so sew
your way and never stray, your father
will lead the way.

    Happy Birthday
      TO: My big brother Lee
         Love Always Your Sister Michelle

            BY: MICHELLE TOSTER
              (a.k.a.) tammy
                4/23/99

IT'S YOUR BIRTHDAY

Happy birthday
today is your day
for which you were
over a year ago, and I can truly say.

That each year
you become more wiser
with wisdom you have pass
down your knowledge to me both
good bad.

If I had to say
you're who I admire
and today is special for
you because your funny, no one can
take this rainbow of joy away.

BY: MICHELLE TOSTER
(a.k.a.) tammy
6/17/94

THE TUNE SPINNER

I knew
a man, a melody man
who once was a prodigy child.

Whom could grasp
anything that was place
in front of him.

I use to say
he's just a philosopher
if one would ask me now I would
tell them he's a navigator.

When he chants
his words were pulverizing
to the soul, "need it be rhythm, blues or
jazz."

The artist my bro
has enthusiasm the sounds
of beening a musician, one could say
he's the pilot of soul; he's my tune spinner
spinning his way surpassing above and
beyond.

Any sounds that blow in the winds
so spin my tune spinner.

BY: MICHELLE TOSTER
(a.k.a.) tammy
6/15/99

CAN YOU HANDLE THE TRUTH /CAN YOU?

If you ask
I'll have to say
don't ask me for things
I can't give.

But if you ask
for love from deep
inside here these things
you can relate to and share.

Most people want the
untouchable, the unreachable
me just give me peace and the rest will
follow.

If the heart isn't cold
and hollow, speak in a soft
slow voice "this makes you easy
so people will ask for many things
that they wouldn't give.

BY: MICHELLE TOSTER
(a.k.a.) tammy
6/17/99

MY HEAVENLY CHILDREN

MR. Clouds
why are you always shifting,
MRS. Sun
your smile gives me joy.

MR. Moon
if you never knew why you keep
coming through.

See my heavenly
child, you are my today
yesterday and always my tomorrow.

You pass by me
each day and nite
and the things you gave me was such a
delight.

I wanted to just let you know
and to say thanks for a life this
great that shines through the heavenly
gates.

BY: MICHELLE TOSTER
(a.k.a.) tammy
6/28/99

THE BLACK MAN (DAD)

You are a black man
I see you as you are, your a part
of four years of history and mystery.

You're the beginning
of my civilization, and my children are the
creators
of your off spring.

You are a black man
you have stood the test of time
you have devastated the world with your
mind.

And I see you you're
big you're small you're bad, you're proud in
all you are
a black man.

Within your soul comes the midst
of a storm, still you're calm, you have
fallen down and yes
you will rise.

I have watched you move forward
toward liberation, and now you will
never stand in the shadows of others.

My father you're free
cause you have cast a shadow of your own
you are a black man, standing strong and
proud at last.

MY FATHER ELZIE ELLIS YOU ARE A BLACK MAN.

BY: MICHELLE TOSTER
(a.k.a.) tammy
2/20/99

A SPECIAL LIFE ISN'T THIS WHAT YOU WANTED AND WISHED FOR?

A special life
if it's all that great
then why do you throw off these things that
great.?

Why when times
are good you wish
them bad? asking yourself
over and over for things you really don't
want.

If and when
the time come to share
a gift of sweet and pure happiness
than why trade the bad for the ugly?

I could would, use to say
if I could make this world a better place
of all that was sweet of sugar and spice
things
will be joyful and nice.

BY: MICHELLE TOSTER
(a.k.a.) tammy
5/30/89

119

JEROME

Jerome
one of God's gifts of the world
one could say that the look in your eyes
could bring tears.

I use to say, that "that was fear
but now I know it's a glaze, a refuge
cause to release all that attitude would
bring forth a war.

I say to you "you're my brother
you're like zenith the highest point of
light
right below the heavens, so you are a
special force.

So chief your the sparkle
in my eyes, so look a yonder cause
within you
there's a winner, and your presence is felt
and feared by
many.

Look in the mirror today
as if it was your last of a new beginning
look to the hills
God will lead you to your liberation but
first you has to
go on this horizon keep in mind, that you
are in peace and any
thing in life can be yours.

MY BRO
WHO HAS the power to bring back what ever as
been stolen

throw off all what's inside your soul and
stand tall be
cool and behold what was lost is to be
found, most of all
carry that special love.

BY: MICHELLE TOSTER
(a.k.a.) tammy
2/23/99

           * LET'S SAVE YOURS*
LET'S SAVE MINE'S*
LET'S SAVE OUR HOME*

           To look the world over
and see nothing but poverty and greeve.

To know that people
use to take care of our mother land.

The generations
was made from sand, and bones
which brought fourth the workers of the
land.

As time went by
the children of our anstories
felt like, why work the land when
the land can work for us.

But they got greedy
they took more than their share
if you look around all you'll see is the
emptions of an unfinish
hopeless world.

I use to say
we can bring back our beautiful, sweet
gentle earth,
but still the world cry's out stop you're
killing us please
take time to look around to see what we have
missed or left out.

Cry not for today, cry for tomorrow, cry for
these days to
come shout it loud, speak it clear, for this
is our home for

which was given as a gift.

The gift of ever lasting love
is this the way we thank our creator
for which is our life, he gave us peace
and joy
for which this world has lost a far to
long ago
pray to restore our home for which has been
destroyed a far
long ago.

BY: MICHELLE TOSTER
(a.k.a.) tammy
6/17/99

WE WERE UNTOUCHABLE

Back in the days
when the trees had more leaves
two or more years ago we could feel
comfortable
and free.

Time took over
our dreams, our hopes, our lives
see I'm asking why can't we be unmoveable
like the mountain next to a ocean shore.

These are the times
when most can't trust their
love or feelings for another because
there's too much bull.

But really all I need is happiness
peace and love this is really, truly the
souls cure.

BY: MICHELLE TOSTER
(a.k.a.) tammy
6/17/99

WHAT IS IT?

You ask you want
for love.

You say you are in
need of joy.

I've asked you
many times before.

What is it?
that your soul
reaches for.

I want a book
which can teach
me all that's needed
to know.

That's all
so I say write your book your own book, of
life for so
as long as it reads treat others as if you
wishes to be treated
give yourself and of yourself let this book
be of all the
good times and dreams then pray and this
book will lead the
way.

BY: MICHELLE TOSTER
(a.k.a.) tammy
6/27/99

MICHAEL

Michael
you're one of God's angels
beautiful, and astounding.

What I'm trying to say
is the life you have should be shared.

With those who care
your soul give off a rare glow.

This love could bring down
a mountain, so use that ingenious
mind.

Keep on keeping on and keep
your mind and your soul in place
and let the lord do the rest, because you're
my bro the best.

BY: MICHELLE TOSTER
(a.k.a.) tammy
2/20/99

* A LOVELY GARDEN GROWS IN YOU *

See you're like a baby
desending sadly side to side, not sure if
you're ready to walk
to me you seem to be like a bud from a sweet
young tree not yet
in bloom.

Most would say it's today it's time to leap
from the root from which you came, with time
it's like a frame
a frame of mind, with you just wanting to be
still; you must know
by now to move ahead and pull yourself from
the soil from which
you hold tight.

You must know that there's nothing but dead
branches and old trees.
I've took a long look, a hard look am most
sure that your heart is
sure and the soul is pure.

Only you hold the true key
to unhook the water which pours out the
years to come this
is your future; the if and when you water
your seed all this is
in the heart of you.

The mind of the flower, will know it's truly
time to stand
up and grow, to grow is to bloom, to sprout
is to go fourth
to bloom is to glow, and these things are
missing from your eyes.

So my flower of sorrow
and of lonely grace; stand-up and take your
place, the world
is yours your garden and you my flower is
the brightest of them
all,

All once more this is your call
stand up and take on all of them look around
you won't bend nor will you fall; remove
those weeds
and go and become free with freedom.

BY: MICHELLE TOSTER
TO: Nioka Ms. Nioka
6/18/00

A BEAUTIFUL LOVE

Auntie Burt
who was a angel
from above.

For when she spoke
your heart would light up
with rays from a rainbow.

Her spirits
elevated you so high
that your soul could dance
across the skies.

She leaves love
that will always last.

Above all my beautiful love
who possess eternal love my sweet
heavenly angel these tears are a cry
of joy "joy my love" now rest my beautiful
love.

BY: MICHELLE TOSTER
(a.k.a.) Tammy Ellis
8/15/99

THE SPECIAL THINGS IN LIFE I LIKE

To have a special life
you must be from a special place
or carrie a special gift of love for the
world.

See it's a special
thing to know this is special
and to show it or to grow with it.

Look around, these are some of my special
things
It's the darkness greenest trees, the clouds,
the skies filled
with big wavey clouds the sun when she
shines.

Not to hot not to cold, and all of the
earth's surrounding
moving, singing doing the work of our
father.

Just pure spearding
out that special word that special
love which carrie nothing but joy.

BY: MICHELLE TOSTER
(a.k.a.) tammy
4/18/87

Printed in the United States
By Bookmasters